Teachers' notes

The uninviting black screen of many Logo programs is often off-putting for both teacher and pupil. Yet once the basics have been grasped a whole world of creativity is unleashed. Logo provides an ideal opportunity to experience two of the most avoided areas of IT in the primary classroom: control – through simple programming using the computer language known as Logo; and modelling – through the almost addictive creative experimentation children rapidly undertake. Put together with its ability to draw on many disciplines – mathematics, language, geography and art to mention a few – its absence from any classroom would be a loss of some magnitude.

The aims of this book

The aims of this book are:
- to explore turtle geometry;
- to provide activities that introduce and consolidate basic Logo commands;
- to develop logical and accurate thought processes;
- to develop problem solving strategies;
- to encourage investigative work and explore the 'what would happen if' scenarios;
- to encourage independent learning;
- to support the non-specialist teacher.

What is Logo?

Logo is a powerful computer programming language that is surprisingly easy to learn. Its user-friendly nature will encourage even the youngest child who will quickly experience its powerful potential. It is an ideal vehicle to explore aspects of geometry, shape and space, symmetry, co-ordinates, simple algebra and number patterns.

However, Logo also has powerful potential in language work. After all Logo is primarily a language. Much can be learned from the precise nature of Logo. When using Logo commands, we are in effect giving the turtle directions, and pupils will soon realise that these instructions need to be accurate and within the language parameters set by Logo (these may differ slightly with different versions of Logo).

Pupils' investigative and explorative work can also generate valuable language work. Many children may, at first, find it difficult to verbalise their findings, but with guidance pupils can be helped to use appropriate vocabulary, write sequentially with accuracy and use language to express causality and prove/disprove hypothesis, using appropriate constructions in their writing.

Once pupils are empowered they can explore and experience Logo in a way which will be highly motivating and in this way Logo will prove to be a tool for further learning experiences in other areas of their work.

Progression

The worksheets are progressively ordered. However, this does not mean they have to be systematically completed in this order. Factors such as pupil experience and success rate need to be taken into account. For example, if a child is finding the concepts of procedures difficult, moving on to superprocedures too quickly would be a mistake. Further consolidation work on procedures would be needed.

Which version of Logo?

There are different versions of Logo which on the whole vary only in syntax. Most schools find that due to variations in purchasing policies they have more than one version of Logo, which they consider to be no more than a minor annoyance. The version of Logo used in this book is RM Logo, although those using BBC will find few problems.

Organisation

The worksheets do not indicate groupings and it is up to the teacher to decide whether a task is dealt with in a group situation or individually.

To help with the smooth running of computer-based sessions pupils need to be familiar with the following basic tasks: loading Logo; closing Logo; saving their work; recalling their work; printing their work.

'Help' cards printed and displayed clearly around the workstation should help with the above.

The worksheets aim to provide a range of activities that are of three types: computer-based; desk-based; either.

The activities would be best introduced to the class as a whole, with the computer-based activities undertaken on a rota basis. It is expected that each computer-based activity will take not more than 30 minutes. While this is a discretionary time-limit, it will deter 'computer dawdling'. It would also be a good idea to photocopy on to card (or paper) computer-based activities that do not require an individual written response, and laminate them so that they can be reused by all pupils. Individual printouts are not always necessary but would on occasion prove useful for pupil records, with perhaps a class-book of 'Logo Activities', containing particularly interesting and successful examples of work (labelled with name and date and including command lines).

When transferring grid work to the screen each vertical and horizontal space between dots represents 10 Logo units and diagonal spaces represent 15 Logo units.

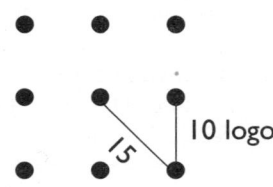

Notes on individual activities

Page 6: Making a turtle turner

Key skills: To learn how to use the turtle turner as an aid to working out Logo turn commands.
The task: The turtle turner is a simple tool which works out right and left turns in 45 degree steps. If children are unfamiliar with 45 and 90 degree angles, an introductory discussion explaining these would bring meaning to the turn commands. Some pupils may need to use it for other activities and this should be encouraged, although eventually it is hoped pupils will be able to work without it.

Page 7: Logo first commands

Key skills: To demonstrate knowledge and application of right and left turns made up of differing multiples of 45 degree angles.
The task: Using the dotted grid on the activity sheet, children follow the sequence of Logo commands. If pupils wish to use their turtle turner this would be acceptable. At the end of the activity the children should have drawn an arrow pointing to the left.

Page 8: Logo secret codes

Key skills: To practise basic Logo commands – fd, bk, rt 90, lt 90, lift and drop.
The task: In this activity children follow the Logo commands in order to decode the message. Some children may need to use their turtle turner to help them establish whether a turn is right or left. If the message has been decoded correctly it should read, 'The treasure is at the end of the rainbow'.

Page 9: Logo squares

Key skills: To practise fd, bk, rt, lt, and repeat commands.
The task: Children need to draw four identical squares each with a different command line. You may need to explain to the children that each 1cm space on their activity sheet needs to be programmed as 10 Logo units. Thus, fd 4 on the grid should be written as fd 40 in the program. As well as developing basic skills, this activity should help children begin to appreciate that there is often more than one solution to a problem.

Page 10: Initials

Key skills: To practise writing a simple drawing program for own initials after first planning on a dotted grid.
The task: The children first draw their initials in the grids provided. They can then use these to work out their programs. Explain that curly initials, such as S and J, will have to resemble digital displays. Emphasise the importance of testing programs to see if the desired result has been achieved and encourage children to 'track down' any errors.

Page 11: Untouchables

Key skills: To plan, write and test simple shape programs; to practise using lift/drop commands.
The task: Children first plan the shapes on their activity sheets and then test their programs at the computer. You may need to explain to children how to position the turtle inside the outer shape without drawing lines, using the lift/drop commands. When colouring the picture, they will need to place the turtle inside the shape. Remember: if shapes are not enclosed colour will spill out of the shape.

Page 12: A simple procedure

Key skills: To write and test a simple procedure; to demonstrate knowledge of fill/colour command.
The task: Introduce children to the fact that a meaningful set of commands can be grouped together to form a procedure. The picture provided is a simple one, involving only 45 and 90 degree turns. However, you may need to explain that the picture is symmetrical, meaning line dimensions will have to be co-ordinated. No starting point has been given to allow children to choose for themselves. When colouring in the lamp, children will need to add in a line to contain the colour. If anyone has written an incorrect procedure, prompt them to try again or to discuss their procedure with someone else.

Page 13: Repeat

Key skills: To identify core commands and rewrite a program using repeat.
The task: In this activity pupils have to identify core commands and count the number of times these are repeated. Once this is done they are ready to write the program using repeat. Explain that they will need to use square brackets and include a space between repeat and the following input. The first, third and fourth drawings can in fact be repeated any number of times but the second drawing is enclosed so the children will need to work out the appropriate number of repeats. The answers are as follows:
repeat 3 [fd 40 rt 90 fd 40 lt 90];
repeat 4 [fd 35 rt 90 fd 35 rt 90 fd 35 lt 90];
repeat 3 [fd 22 rt 90 fd 22 rt 90 fd 22 lt 90 fd 22 lt 90];
repeat 5 [fd 12 rt 135 fd 12 lt 135]
repeat 5 [fd 44 bk 44 rt 10] If this one is repeated 36 times it will form a circle.

Page 14: Co-ordinate moves

Key skills: Positioning the turtle on the screen using co-ordinates; developing use of the setpos and stamp commands.
The tasks: Pupils need to be introduced to the 'setpos' command. The 'setpos' command enables the turtle to be sent to a position on the screen in one movement. This activity provides a good opportunity to encourage the use of negative numbers in the children's programs and the effects

these make on the outcome of the programs. When stamping the turtle shapes in the quadrants, children need to think about the symmetry involved. When finished they should study the co-ordinates and see if they can notice a pattern.

Page 15: Logo bowls

Key skills: Estimating lengths and rotations; changing turtle shape; stamping image of the turtle.
The task: Photocopy this sheet on to a piece of acetate, or trace it on to overhead projector paper, and position it in front of the computer screen with tape. The children place their turtle in the box on the sheet. In pairs they take it in turn to try and send their turtle inside one of the pins. If they are successful they stamp their turtle's image on to that pin. (Each child should choose a different turtle shape.) When choosing a turtle shape, encourage pupils to choose small ones which will fit inside the pins. Whoever manages to stamp most pins wins.

Page 16: Pathways

Key skills: To develop skills of estimation and calculation of angles; to practise using the rubber facility.
The task: The following procedure needs to be saved and named 'path'.
rt 90 fd 60 lt 90 fd 20 lt 90 fd 60 lt 90 fd 100 lt 90 fd 60 lt 90 fd 80
This procedure will draw the picture found on the worksheet. Children can recall it by simply keying in the word 'path'. Pupils will gain much from trial and error techniques, which can later be refined with teacher input so that mathematical knowledge is applied where appropriate.

Page 17: Regular polygons

Key skills: Writing programs based on a general formula.
The task: A class introduction to this activity could be divided into two parts. The first dealing with the properties of regular polygons and the associated mathematics, the second dealing with the actual command line proposed in the general formula. Explain to the children that Logo will divide for them and the forward slash symbol stands for divide. For each program the children should repeat and divide the polygon by the number of sides that polygon has. So, for example, the formula for a heptagon will be **repeat 7 [fd 40 rt 360/7]**. The two questions at the end will test children's understanding of the formula and will help in identifying those who are just following the formula and those who are grasping the concepts involved. In the formula, 40 could be changed to any other number as it determines the size of the regular polygon without altering the shape. The final question relates to the fact that regular polygons have equal sides and angles and there are 360 degrees in a full turn.

Page 18: Curves and circles

Key skills: Generating curves and circles of varying sizes using only fd and rt/lt commands.
The task: This task is suitable both for children who are aware of the circle generating command and those who are not. It is based on exploring the properties of circles and curves. Hopefully, children will appreciate the fact that a circle is made up of infinitely small sides. Using the formula as a guide, children should come to understand that **repeat 360 [fd 1 rt 1]** will produce a circle. At this stage, ways of making their circles smaller should be explored, with children predicting the outcomes before testing. Do not forget numbers smaller than 1. This provides an excellent opportunity to observe Logo's ability to calculate **repeat 360 [fd 1/6 rt 1]** The sentences regarding different-sized circles could be written in the form of a rule. Which inputs need to stay constant? Which inputs vary the size? Why? You may need to explain that the fd size needs to be different as this determines the size of the circle or semicircle. A solution to the pattern is given:
lt 180
repeat 180 [fd 1/2 lt 1]
repeat 180 [fd 1/8 rt 1]
repeat 180 [fd 1/5 rt 1]

Page 19: Logo faces

Key skills: Drawing circles and curves; positioning the turtle on screen.
The task: Children will need to apply their findings from the previous worksheet 'Curves and circles' in order to write this procedure. It may be a useful exercise to ask children to work out the size of circle needed for each part of the face. After this they will need to work out the best way to position their turtle. The setpos command may be an option here (you may like to refer the children back to the worksheet 'Co-ordinate moves' on page 14).

Page 20: Repeat patterns

Key skills: To produce repeating designs; calculating the x and y values in the formula given.
The task: This task is based around repeating and rotating a procedure based on a formula given. While the formula in itself does not demand a full turn, pupils should be asked to aim for this when making their own patterns. The answers to the questions are as follows: 36; 30; if you wish to make a full turn of 360 then y must be divided by x enough times to make 360. This third question, in fact, is based on the premise that a full turn is made and the previous two questions support this. All procedures are made by accessing the edit box, which is done by the build command followed by an apostrophe and the name of the procedure, for example **build 'face**.

Page 21: De-bugging

Key skills: To test and de-bug programs.
The task: Pupils are asked to test programs and de-bug them so that they produce the necessary results (shown in the sketches). The whole process should be one that the children accept as part of the overall task, as necessary as any other and as valued as any other. It should never be seen as 'extra' and if approached in this way should not demoralise pupils. The correct solution to the sketches shown are as follows:
repeat 4 [fd 44 rt 90];
fd 30 rt 90 fd 60 lt 90 fd 33;
repeat 6 [fd 50 rt 60];
lt 90 fd 33 rt 135 fd 66 lt 135 fd 44

Page 22: Variables

Key skills: Writing a procedure with a variable length input.
The task: Children will need to be introduced to the notion of variable inputs and the advantages of these. They can follow the framework for square when writing their own procedure for a hexagon. Their procedure shoud read:
hexagon 'side
repeat 6 [fd :side rt 360/6]
end
Allow pupils to consult their previous work if they wish. When drawing shapes of different sizes, encourage children to explore negative numbers also. The command line at the bottom of the page incorporates the variable input procedures with the inclusion of repeat. Pupils are asked to explore this command line. Before testing the program, pupils should be encouraged to first 'guess' what will happen and then change input values – first by trial and error and hopefully later by building relationships. At first children may find it difficult to verbalise their findings but with encouragement, help and practice the task will become easier. Ask pupils to come up with 'if' 'then' and 'because' statements. For example, 'If I rotate my hexagon by 10 degrees, I shall have to repeat it 36 times to complete my design because there are 360 degrees in a full turn.' When children have built up their confidence, ask them to form and later test their own hypothesis.

Page 23: Tessellating regular polygons

Key skills: Using procedures with variable inputs.
The task: The key to tessellating the octagons and squares is to get the turtle facing the right direction before drawing either shape. The following are two possible procedures for the octagon and the square.
octagon: repeat 8 [fd 44 rt 360/8]
square: repeat 4 [fd 44 rt 90]
As both the above procedures use a right turn (they could have used a left) this must be considered when positioning the turtle. Knowledge of the internal and external angles of the octagon will also be useful. Note: 360/8 gives the external angle, the internal angle of the octagon is 135 (360/8 = 45 (180 – 45 = 135)) The tessellation will only work if the sides of the hexagon and square are the same.

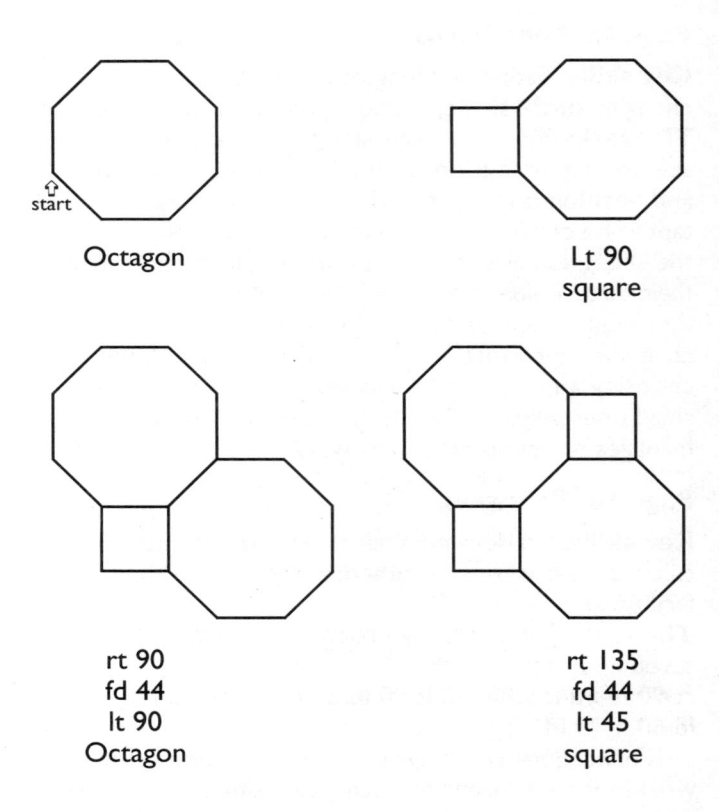

Octagon

Lt 90
square

rt 90
fd 44
lt 90
Octagon

rt 135
fd 44
lt 45
square

Page 24: Varying angles

Key skills: To write a variable input procedure.
The task: Pupils are given the basic command line for drawing a 45 degree angle. They must then access the edit box and make it into a procedure, replacing the 45 with a variable input. The worksheet 'Variables' on page 22 should provide children with the framework required to find a solution for themselves.
Solution: build 'myangle to access edit box. Then:
myangle 'angle
fd 60 bk 60 rt :angle fd 60 bk 60
end
A possible program to create the design would be repeat 36 [myangle 10].
The explanation at the end needs to revolve around the relationship between the number of repeats and the size of rotation. An acceptable rotation will be anywhere between 5 and 20. Children should compare work and discuss outcomes. Did everyone make one full turn or did some make more? Why was this? After one full turn does the pattern change? The final question on the activity sheet relates to the relationship between the repeats and the number of turns. The smaller the angle the closer the lines will be together.

Page 25: Sam's journey

Key skills: To investigate different solutions; to map out paths using Logo commands.
The task: Pupils need to work with the map 'Sam's journey' and work out appropriate routes to the various destinations given on the sheet. The fuel restraint is a very important one. Sam's car needs to be refuelled every 15 km. Pupils need to work out for themselves when and where to refuel on a particular journey. The step from the dot into the place being visited also counts for 1 km. Sam's car will first need to go to the petrol station in order to refuel. This is 5 km away. He can just make it to the petrol station before his car runs out of petrol.

Page 26: Procedures with variable inputs

Key skills: To write procedures with variable inputs.
The task: Pupils write procedures with variable inputs and use these to create repeating designs. This activity reinforces the work children have been doing in side and angle variables. Note that a rectangle requires two inputs as it has two different-sized sides.

Page 27: Parallelogram kite

Key skills: Writing a procedure with a variable input; filling shapes with solid colour; constructing a picture using a procedure.
The task: Pupils need to create a variable input procedure using the program given. In order to construct the picture, pupils need to position different-sized parallelograms.

Page 28: Speed rocket

Key skills: To list co-ordinate points; define new turtle shape; demonstrate knowledge and use of speed and directional changes for the turtle.
The task: To create a new shape for the turtle, pupils need to use the 'defineshape' command. Once this has been done the new shape can be taken up by the turtle using the more commonly-used command: setshape. The first part of the activity sheet is a preparatory task, as defineshape requires a list of co-ordinates of the shape's vertices. To change the turtle into the rocket shape the following command line is needed.
Defineshape [rocket [-5 -10] [-5 0] [-10 0] [-5 10] [-5 15] [0 25] [5 15] [5 10] [10 0] [5 0] [5 -10] [-5 -10] Without the final co-ordinate pair the shape would not be a closed one. Remember: for the turtle to take up the shape the children need to **setshape 'rocket**.

Page 29: Recursion

Key skills: To create recursive procedures.
The task: A recursive procedure is one that uses itself as a sub procedure. The answer to the first question is referring to this. By studying the second picture, children should notice that while some elements of the procedure are repeating (fd and rt 90) there is also a repetitive change (addition of five units on the length). A procedure for a spiral is only possible with this last refinement.

Page 30: A superprocedure!

Key skills: To create a superprocedure by building on sub procedures.
The task: Introduce children to the concept of a superprocedure being a procedure that includes smaller sub procedures. Pupils are asked to create a superprocedure that will draw their name. Writing programs for individual letters should not be a problem. However, pupils need to consider what will happen after they have written their first letter. If they have not considered how each procedure will follow after the other, the letters will not be spaced out appropriately. If adjustments have not been made to incorporate the end or start position of the turtle after each procedure this will be the case. Refer the children back to the activity sheet 'Co-ordinate moves' on page 14 if they need to practise how to move the turtle to a particular place on the screen.

Page 31: Superprocedures

Key skills: Writing a superprocedure.
The task: The picture of the flower has been broken down into five parts. The fifth procedure called 'flower' being the end result. The program for the leaf has been given and this should be used for the petals too. The picture of the flower given has nine petals and pupils should replicate this, working out the repeat and rotation values. When the petals are rotated pupils will need to remember that the turtle will face north every time the procedure named leaf is run. When investigating flower shapes, pupils may be advised to delete the ct command which will allow repeat commands to work more efficiently. The procedures for the different parts of the flower are as follows:
Leaves: Leaf ct repeat 80 [fd 1/2 lt 1]; lt 100; repeat 80 [fd 1/2 lt 1]
Stem: Leaves ct fd 60
Bud: Stem repeat 360 [fd 10 bk 10 rt 1]
Flower: Bud repeat 9 [leaf rt 60]

Page 32: Snow crystals

Key skills: To create sub procedures for a superprocedure called snowflake.
The task: Within the parameters set, pupils should be allowed to be as creative as possible, and trial and error techniques should not be discouraged as these often form the basis of some very worthwhile work. Children should test and de-bug their procedures as they go along rather than waiting until the end.

✸ Name _____

Making a turtle turner

✸ Stick the picture of the turtle turner on to a piece of card and cut it out. Now use it to work out the turns in the box below. Draw in the new positions.

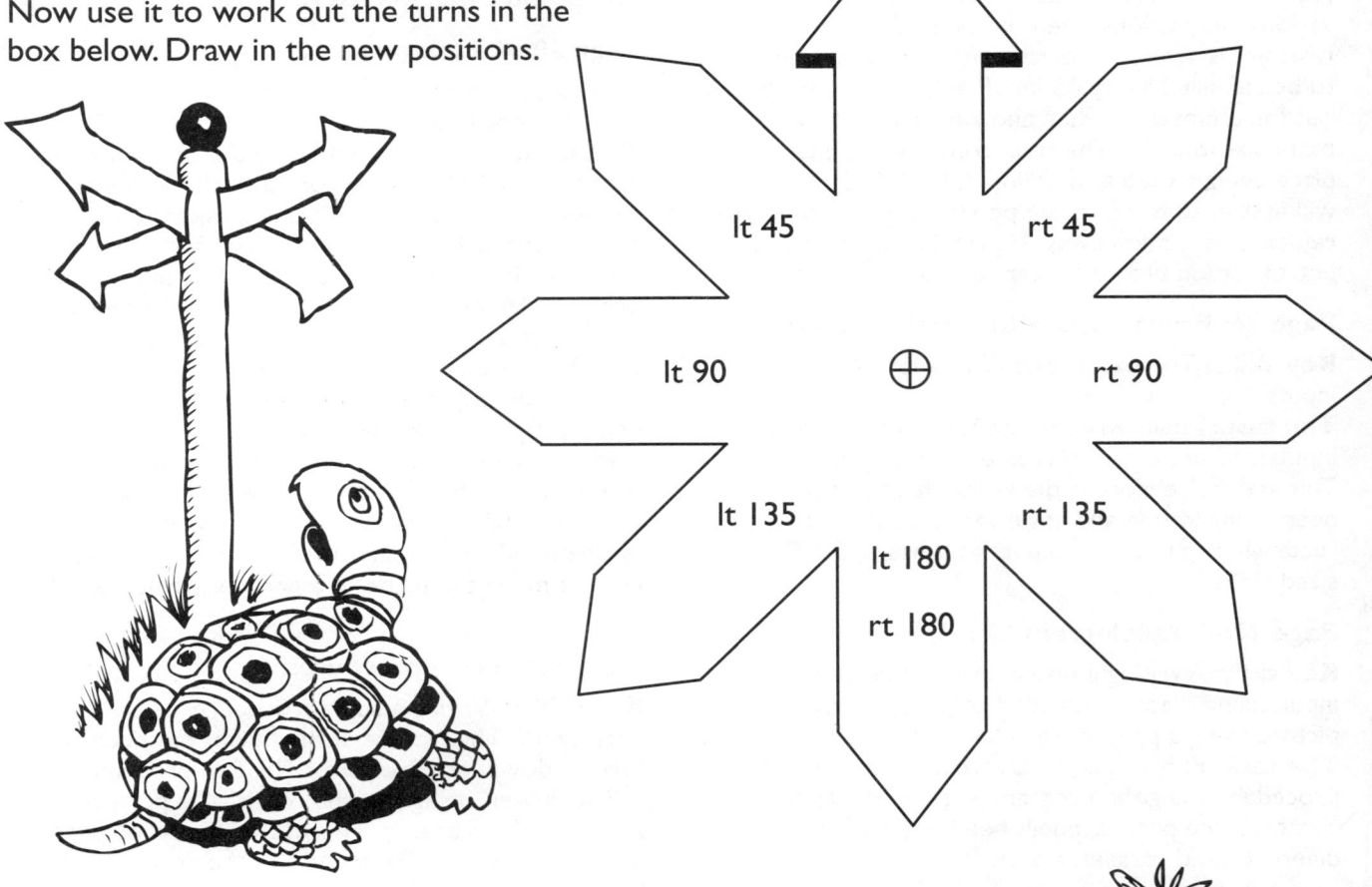

lt 45   rt 45
lt 90   rt 90
lt 135   rt 135
lt 180
rt 180

Starting position	Logo command	New position
⇧	rt 135	
⇦	lt 45	
⇨	lt 180	
⇩	rt 90	
⇨	rt 90	

✸ ESSENTIALS FOR INFORMATION TECHNOLOGY:
Control through Logo

Logo first commands

✹ Follow the Logo instructions at the bottom of the page and draw them on the dotted grid opposite. Show forward and backward moves with straight pencil lines and turns with arrow heads.

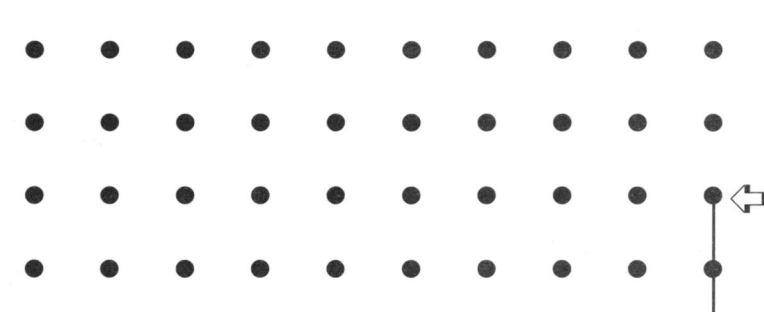

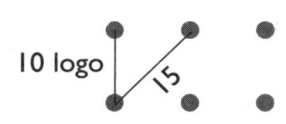

Remember: 10 logo / 15

✹ Tick off each command as you draw it. The first two have been done for you.

⇧ Start

fd 5 ✓	lt 90 ✓	fd 5	rt 90	fd 2
lt 135	fd 4	lt 90	fd 4	lt 135
fd 3	rt 90	fd 4	rt 90	fd 4

What have you drawn? _____

ESSENTIALS FOR INFORMATION TECHNOLOGY:
Control through Logo

✸ Name _____

Logo secret codes

✸ Decode the message below by following the Logo commands. Note where the turtle lands each time.

| fd 5 | bk 3 | bk 2 rt 90 fd 2 |

___ ___ ___

| bk 2 lt 90 fd 5 | bk 5 rt 90 fd 5 | bk 3 | bk 3 | fd 1 rt 90 fd 5 |

___ ___ ___ ___ ___

| bk 5 rt 90 fd 6 | bk 11 | fd 3 | | bk 1 | fd 3 lt 90 fd 5 |

___ ___ ___   ___ ___

| bk 5 rt 90 fd 1 | bk 1 rt 90 fd 5 | | lift drop | bk 3 | bk 2 rt 90 fd 2 |

___ ___   ___ ___ ___

| lift drop | fd 2 | bk 4 rt 90 fd 1 | | fd 3 | bk 4 rt 90 fd 2 |

___ ___ ___   ___ ___

✸ Using the above Logo decoder, write your own secret message to a friend.

| bk 2 rt 90 fd 5 | bk 3 | bk 2 rt 90 fd 2 |

___ ___ ___

| fd 3 | bk 6 | fd 4 | fd 1 | bk 3 | bk 1 rt 90 fd 4 | fd 2 |

___ ___ ___ ___ ___ ___ ___

✸ ESSENTIALS FOR INFORMATION TECHNOLOGY:
Control through Logo

8

✸ Name _____

Logo squares

Remember:

✸ In the grids below draw four 5 by 5 squares. Each one needs to have a different set of Logo commands. Write the commands in the spaces under each grid. When you have finished try them out on the computer.

15 / 10 logo

1.

2.

3.

4.

ESSENTIALS FOR INFORMATION TECHNOLOGY:
Control through Logo

✹ Name _____

Initials

At your desk
✸ Using the dots as guides, draw your first two initials in the grids below. Write a program for drawing each initial.

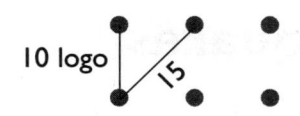

Remember: 10 logo / 15

At the computer
✸ Test your programs.

My program
_____
_____
_____
_____
_____
_____
_____
_____
_____
_____

My program
_____
_____
_____
_____
_____
_____
_____
_____
_____

✹ ESSENTIALS FOR INFORMATION TECHNOLOGY:
Control through Logo

✻ Name _____

Untouchables

At your desk
✻ Write programs to draw the following sets of shapes. Make sure they do not touch each other.

At the computer
✻ When testing your programs at the computer, colour each shape a different colour.

Remember:

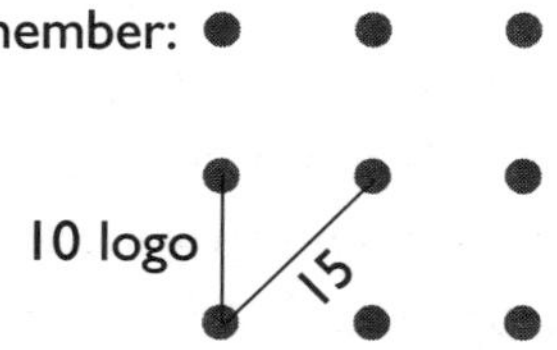

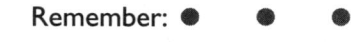

10 logo 15

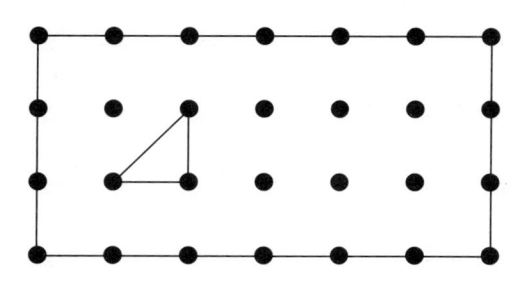

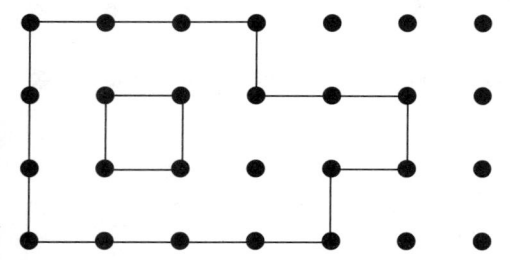

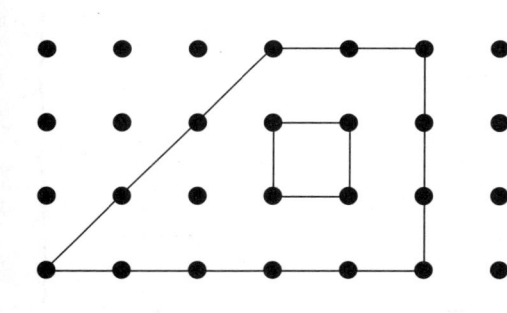

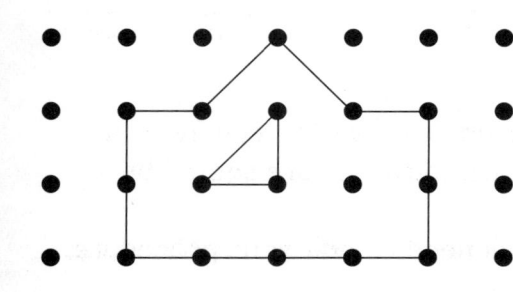

✻ ESSENTIALS FOR INFORMATION TECHNOLOGY:
Control through Logo

11

A simple procedure

At your desk
✹ Write a procedure called 'Lamp' which will draw the picture shown opposite. Write the commands you will use on the lines provided.

At the computer
✹ Key in your procedure in the edit box. Now return to your normal Logo screen. Type in the word 'Lamp' and press Enter. If your procedure is correct, the above picture should be displayed on your screen.
✹ Now colour in your lamp in a colour of your choice. You will need to edit your procedure.

ESSENTIALS FOR INFORMATION TECHNOLOGY:
Control through Logo

Name _____

Repeat

There are times when you have to key in the same commands over and over again. Think about the commands you would need to draw a square.

fd 55 rt 90 fd 55 rt 90 fd 55 rt 90 fd 55 rt 90

If you look carefully, you will notice that two commands are repeated four times. These are **fd 55 and rt 90.** Let's call these the Core Commands. By using the repeat command a lot of time can be saved.

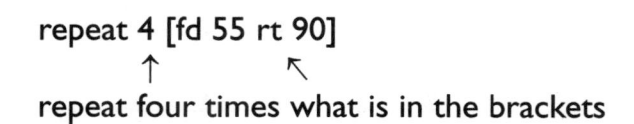

repeat 4 [fd 55 rt 90]
      ↑   ↖
repeat four times what is in the brackets

✹ Identify the Core Commands in the following programs and rewrite them using the repeat command.

	Original command line	New command line
	fd 40 rt 90 fd 40 lt 90 fd 40 rt 90 fd 40 lt 90 fd 40 rt 90 fd 40 lt 90	
	fd 35 rt 90 fd 35 rt 90 fd 35 lt 90 fd 35 rt 90 fd 35 rt 90 fd 35 lt 90 fd 35 rt 90 fd 35 rt 90 fd 35 lt 90 fd 35 rt 90 fd 35 rt 90 fd 35 lt 90	
	fd 22 rt 90 fd 22 rt 90 fd 22 lt 90 fd 22 lt 90 fd 22 rt 90 fd 22 rt 90 fd 22 lt 90 fd 22 lt 90 fd 22 rt 90 fd 22 rt 90 fd 22 lt 90 fd 22 lt 90	
	fd 12 rt 135 fd 12 lt 135 fd 12 rt 135 fd 12 lt 135 fd 12 rt 135 fd 12 lt 135 fd 12 rt 135 fd 12 lt 135 fd 12 rt 135 fd 12 lt 135	
	fd 44 bk 44 rt 10 fd 44 bk 44 rt 10 fd 44 bk 44 rt 10 fd 44 bk 44 rt 10 fd 44 bk 44 rt 10	

✹ ESSENTIALS FOR INFORMATION TECHNOLOGY:
Control through Logo

✹ Name _____

Co-ordinate moves

It is possible to move the turtle without using the fd and bk commands. This is done by positioning the turtle using co-ordinates. The turtle is positioned on the screen by using the setpos command.

Example:
setpos [40 80]

This number refers to the x co-ordinate and tells the turtle how far to the right or left to move. The x co-ordinate is always written first.

This number refers to the y co-ordinate and tells the turtle how far up and down to move. The y co-ordinate is always written last.

✹ Move the turtle around the screen using the setpos command.

✹ In the grid opposite draw a cross in the quadrant where the turtle would be if the command line was **setpos [-40 -80]**

✹ Change the shape and colour of your turtle.

✹ Now stamp the shape of your turtle in each of the four quadrants, making sure they are symmetrical with one another. Record your co-ordinates in the boxes below.

✹ ESSENTIALS FOR INFORMATION TECHNOLOGY:
Control through Logo

Logo bowls

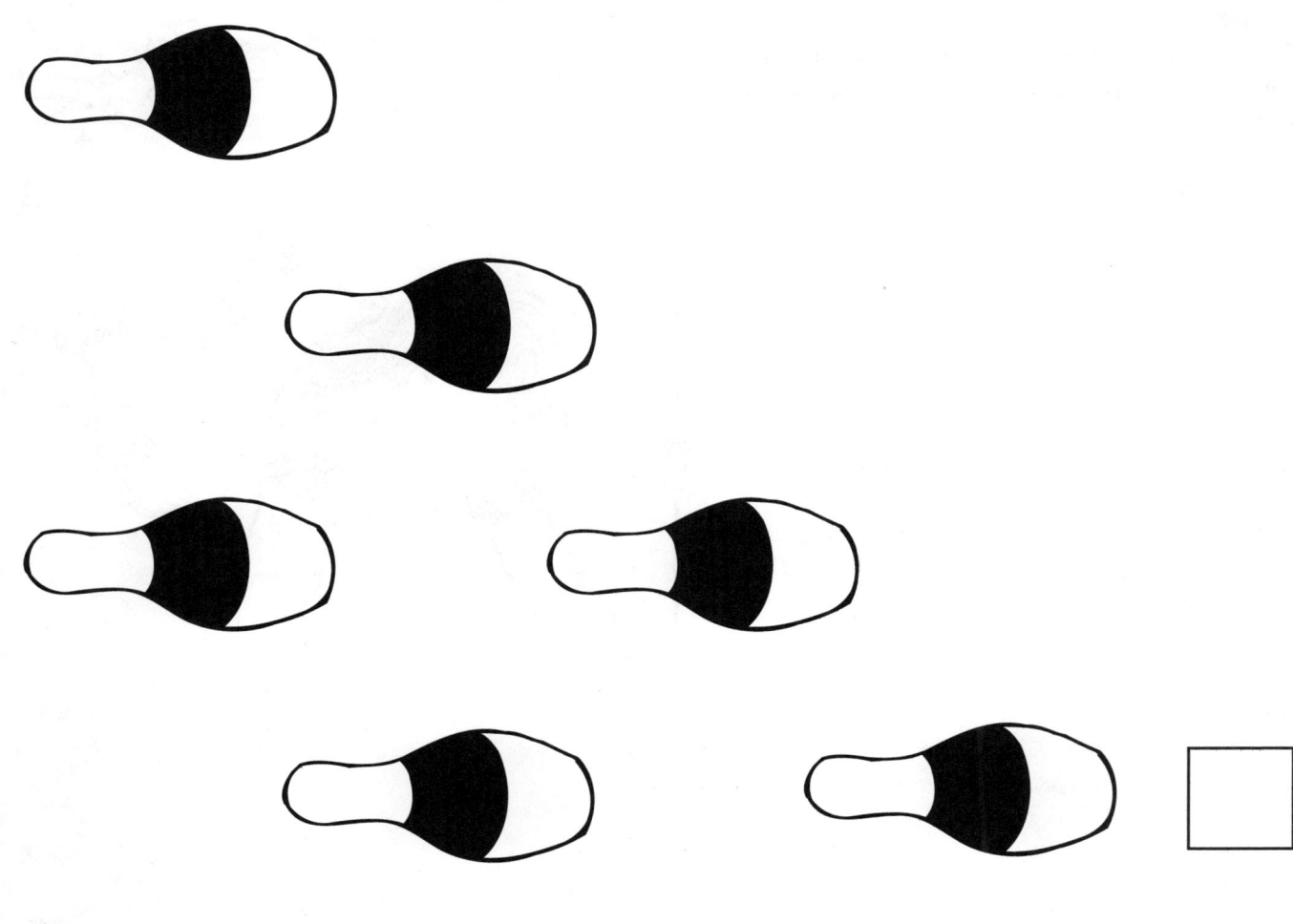

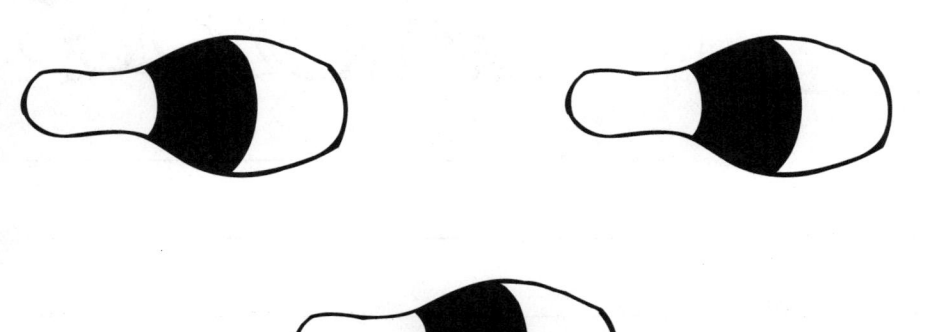

ESSENTIALS FOR INFORMATION TECHNOLOGY:
Control through Logo

Pathways

At your desk
✸ Using a coloured crayon, find a path that will retrace the shape below without going over any line more than once.

At the computer
✸ Key in the word 'path' and press Enter. You will see a shape similar to the one above.

• Change the pen colour of the turtle. Now retrace over the lines of the picture using the path you discovered above. You will need to estimate the length of the sides and 'rub out' any extended lines.

• Write a program of your own that will draw the above shape without going over any lines more than once.

• Test your program.

ESSENTIALS FOR INFORMATION TECHNOLOGY:
Control through Logo

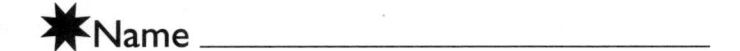

Regular polygons

✸ Use the following formula to write programs for drawing regular polygons.

repeat s [fd 40 rt 360/s]

↑ number of sides polygon has

↑ 360 divided by the number of sides

> A regular polygon is a shape that has three or more straight equal sides and equal angles.

✸ Complete the following table. The first one has been done for you.

Name of regular polygon	Program	Test result
Triangle	repeat 3 [fd 40 rt 360/3]	✓
Square		
Pentagon		
Hexagon		
Heptagon		
Octagon		
Nonagon		
Decagon		
Hendecagon		

In the formula could the unit 40 be exchanged for another number?

_____

Why do you think 360 has to be divided by the number of sides?

_____

Name _____

Curves and circles

It is possible to draw curves and circles very easily using Logo.

✱ Look at the formula used to draw regular polygons.

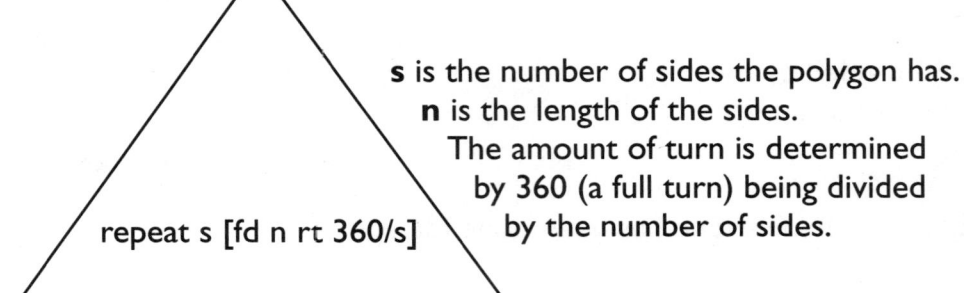

repeat s [fd n rt 360/s]

s is the number of sides the polygon has.
n is the length of the sides.
The amount of turn is determined by 360 (a full turn) being divided by the number of sides.

✱ Do you think the above formula can help you to draw a circle? Give reasons for your answer.

_____

_____

If your answer was no, try thinking of a circle as being a shape with an infinite number of sides which are infinitely small.

✱ Using the above formula, write a program for drawing a circle on a separate piece of paper.

• Now rewrite your program to draw a smaller circle.

• Now write a sentence or two to explain what you have to do to draw different-sized circles.

_____

_____

_____

• Write a program to draw the pattern opposite. It is made up of three different-sized semicircles.

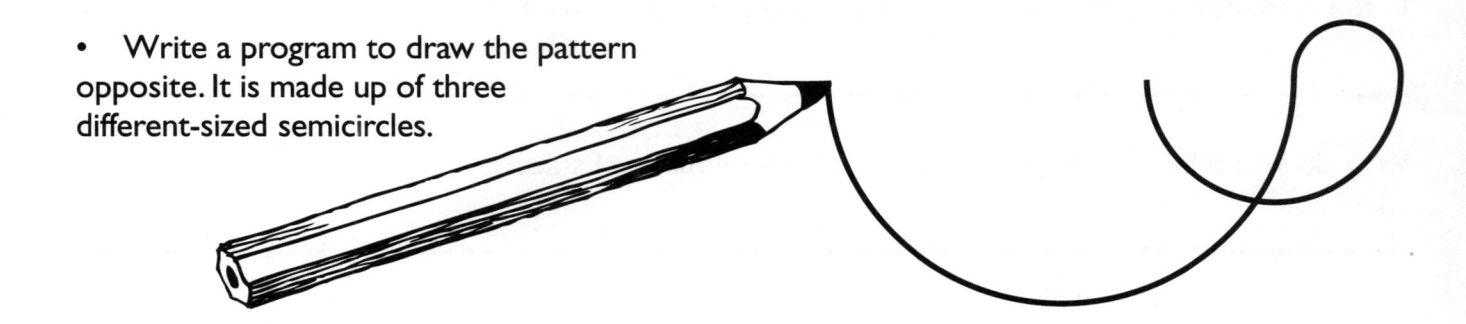

✱ ESSENTIALS FOR INFORMATION TECHNOLOGY:
Control through Logo

✶ Name _____

Logo faces

At the computer
✶ Write a procedure that will draw the large face below. Call your procedure 'happy'.

At your desk
✶ Do some planning here.

_____
_____
_____
_____
_____

Can you edit your procedure to change the expression from happy to sad?
✶ Try creating other facial expressions.

Repeat patterns

✱ Look at the pattern opposite. It was created using the procedure 'octagon'.

Procedure for an octagon:
repeat 8 [fd 55 rt 360/8]

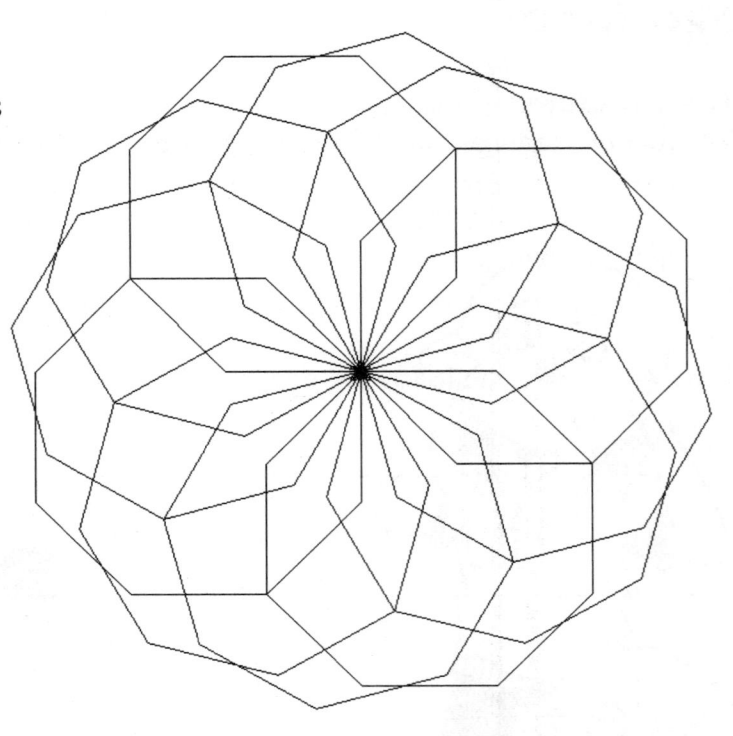

Study the following formula

Repeat x [octagon rt y]

x stands for the number of repeats   y stands for the amount of rotational turn

How many repeats would you need if **y =10** degrees in the formula above and you wanted to complete a full turn? _____

What would be the angle of rotation (**y**) if the procedure 'octagon' was repeated 12 times using the above formula and you wanted to complete a full turn? _____

Can you write a rule which relates to the relationship of x and y?

_____

_____

✱ Test your rule.

✱ Investigate making patterns using the procedure **octagon** and the formula given above.

ESSENTIALS FOR INFORMATION TECHNOLOGY:
Control through Logo

De-bugging

When we write programs we need to test them to make sure they work and that there are no mistakes. If a program does not do what you intended it to do it has to be de-bugged. In other words you have to track down the mistake (or bug!)

✱ Test and de-bug the following programs.

	Program	Test result	Corrected program	Test result 2	Program de-bugged?
▢	repeat 4 [fd 44 rt 900]				
⌐	fd 30 rt 90 fd 60 rt 90 fd 33				
⬡	repeat 6 [fd 6 rt 16]				
Z	fd 33 rt 135 fd 66 lt 135 fd 44				

ESSENTIALS FOR INFORMATION TECHNOLOGY:
Control through Logo

Name _____

Variables

When we write programs for regular polygons we can specify the size of each one. It would be better if we could write a program that was more flexible and let us vary the size of our polygons easily.

✸ Let us write a procedure in the edit box. **build 'square** will take us to the edit box. Here we must write our procedure.

**square 'side
repeat 4 [fd :side rt 90]
end**
↑

We are telling the computer that at the moment we do not know the length of the sides.

✸ Now return to your normal Logo screen.
Key in **square 30** and Enter. Now draw squares of differing sizes.

In this way **square** has become a more useful procedure.

✸ Write a similar procedure for a regular hexagon. _____
_____
_____

✸ Using your new procedure, draw the design below.

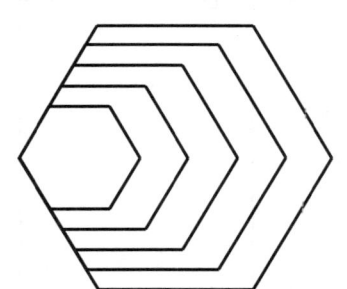

✸ Explore the following program. Before you press Enter try to work out what will happen.

repeat 18 [hexagon 66 rt 20 hexagon 33]

✸ Name _____

Tessellating regular polygons

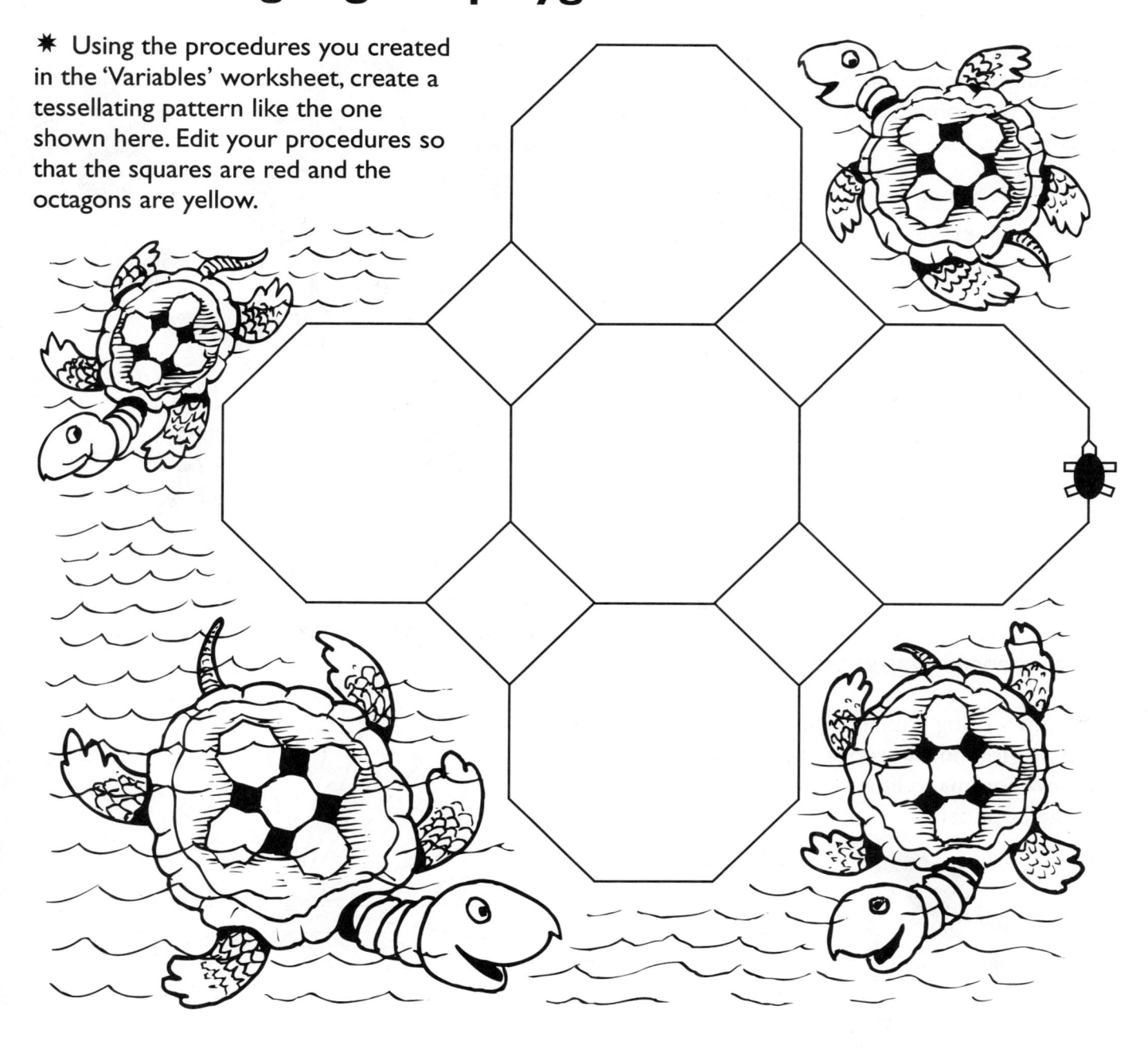

✸ Using the procedures you created in the 'Variables' worksheet, create a tessellating pattern like the one shown here. Edit your procedures so that the squares are red and the octagons are yellow.

How long were the sides of your square? _____ Logo units.

How long were the sides of your octagon? _____ Logo units.

Can you explain these measurements?

✸ Try creating some different tessellations, using at least three different shapes.

✸ ESSENTIALS FOR INFORMATION TECHNOLOGY:
Control through Logo

✳ Name _____

Varying angles

Just as you can have a variable length measurement you can also have a variable angle. This is the command line to draw a 45 degree angle.

    fd 60   **bk 60**
    rt 45   **fd 60**

✳ Now write a procedure in the edit box that will let you draw an angle of any size. Call your procedure **myangle**.

_____

_____

✳ Test your new procedure by drawing different-sized angles. Remember, if your procedure works you will only have to key in **myangle** followed by the size of angle you want to draw. For instance **myangle 60**.

✳ Now using your new procedure called **myangle** and the repeat command, write a new command line that will create the design opposite.

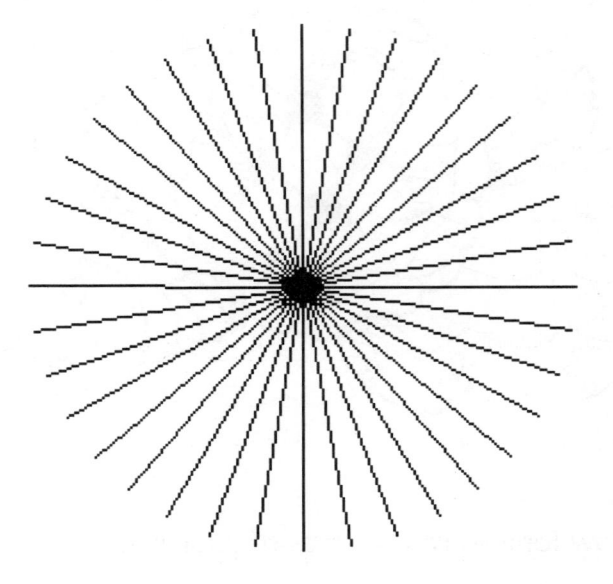

Explain why your command line works. _____

_____

_____

Can you write a program that will draw a coloured circle without using the fill command?

Sam's journey

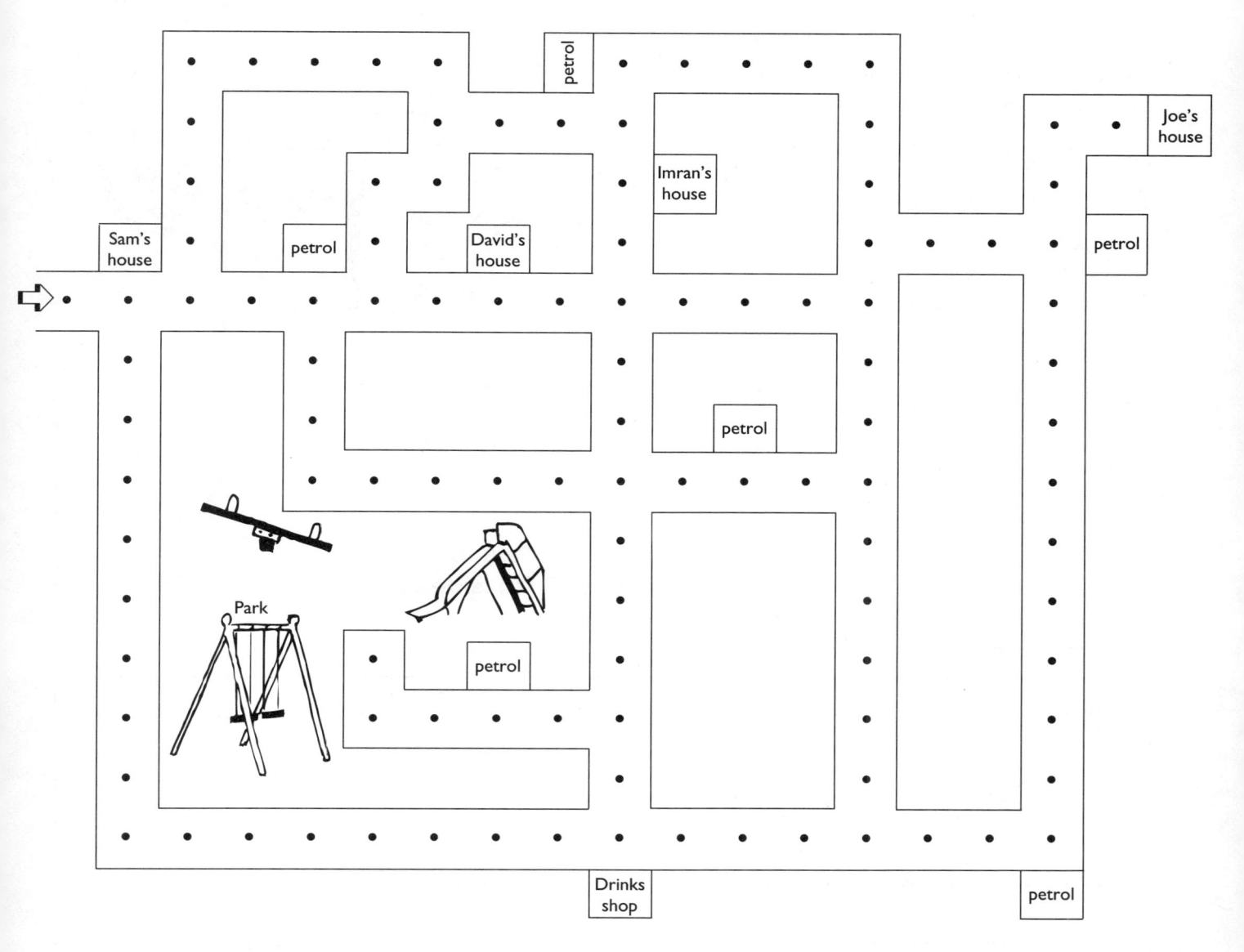

✷ Study the map above. Using Logo commands, investigate the following problems. Write your answers on a separate sheet of paper

Sam's car can only travel 15 km before needing to be refuelled.

1. Sam's car has travelled 10 km already. Where will he need to go next in order to continue his journey?

2. The next journey Sam makes is to his best friend's house, 9 km away. Name Sam's friend.

3. Sam and his friend now go to the park. Record your Logo commands

4. Both Sam and his friend decide to have a drink, where will they go?

5. Now Sam and his friend both decide to visit their friend Joe. Record your Logo commands.

6. After a short visit Sam and his friend decide to return to Sam's home. Give the commands.

Name _____

Procedures with variable inputs

✸ Write procedures with variable inputs for the following shapes. The first one has been done for you.

Shape	Procedure
rec	**rec 'sidea 'sideb** **repeat 2 [fd :sidea rt 90 fd :sideb rt 90]**
vee	
lid	
zig	

✸ Using your procedures, create as many designs as possible.

ESSENTIALS FOR INFORMATION TECHNOLOGY:
Control through Logo

Parallelogram kite

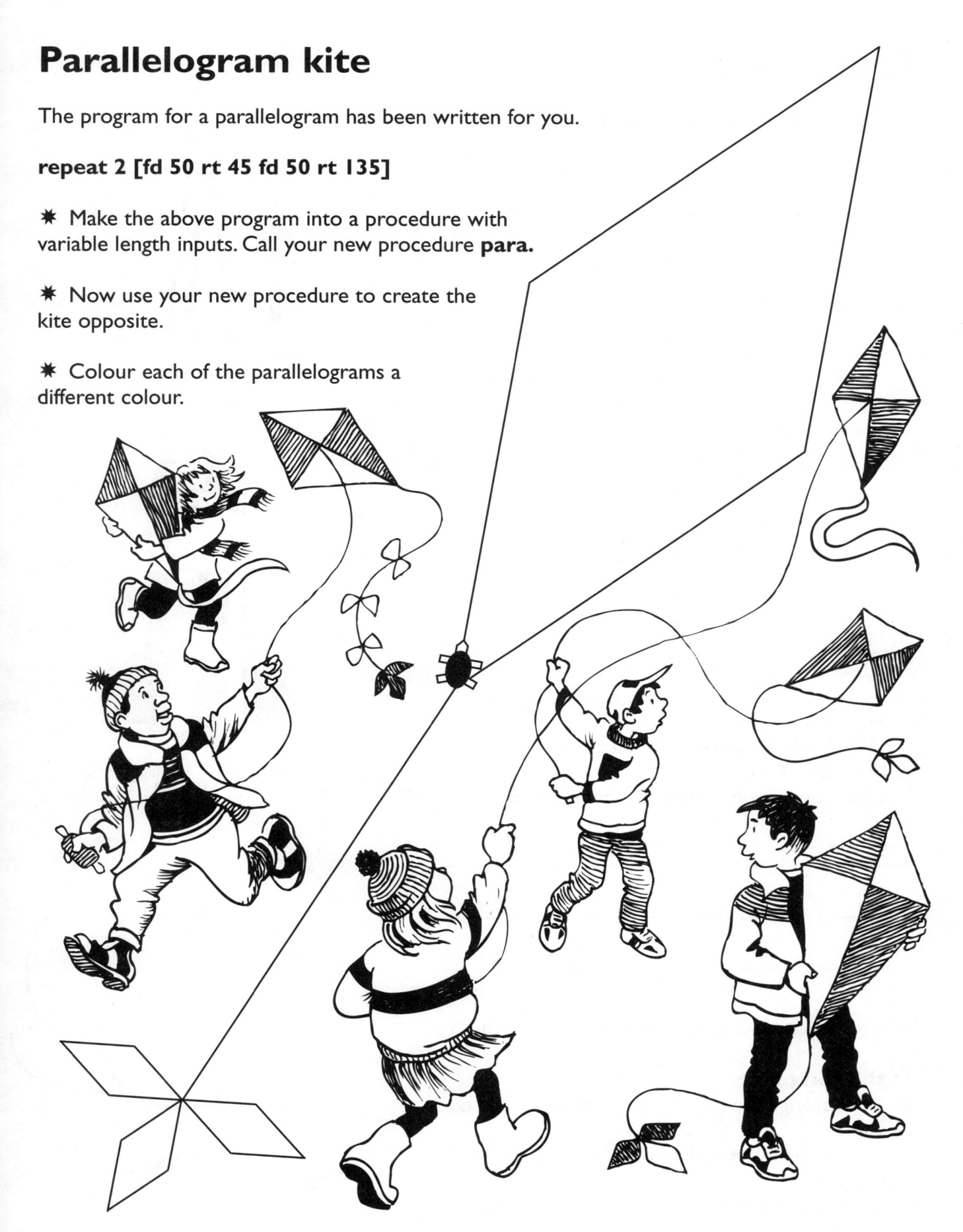

The program for a parallelogram has been written for you.

repeat 2 [fd 50 rt 45 fd 50 rt 135]

✸ Make the above program into a procedure with variable length inputs. Call your new procedure **para.**

✸ Now use your new procedure to create the kite opposite.

✸ Colour each of the parallelograms a different colour.

✱ Name _____

Speed rocket

✱ Look at the picture of a rocket drawn on the grid below.

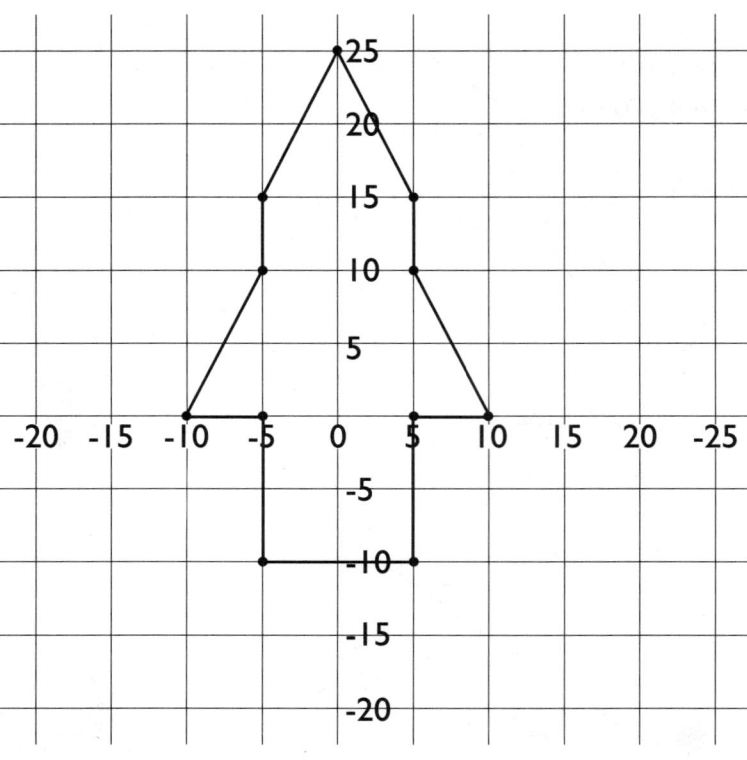

At your desk
✱ Working in a clockwise direction, list the co-ordinates of the vertices.
The first and last one have been done for you.

-5 -10 _____ _____ _____

_____ _____ _____ _____

_____ _____ _____ -5 -10

Why is the last co-ordinate point the same as the first?

At the computer
✱ Now, change the shape of your turtle to the one above.
• Set the turtle's speed to 10. Now watch your rocket take off!
• Experiment with speed and direction changes.

✱ ESSENTIALS FOR INFORMATION TECHNOLOGY:
Control through Logo

✳ Name _____

Recursion

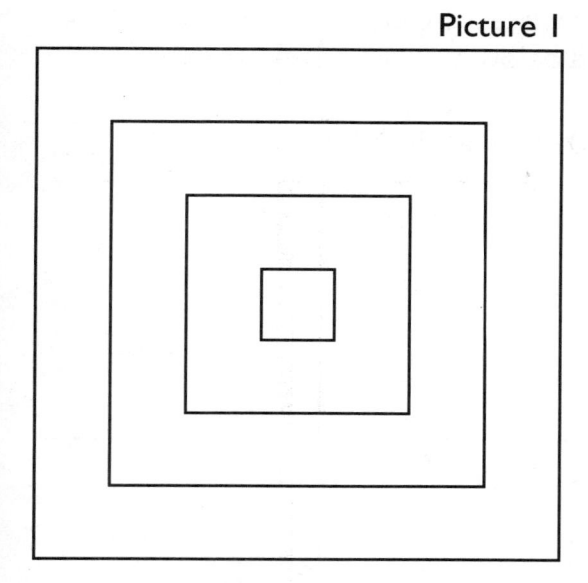

Picture 1

Picture 2

At your desk
✳ Look at the two pictures above. They are similar but not identical.

• Write a sentence to describe how they are different from each other.

_____

_____

• Measure the straight lines in picture 2. Write a sentence to describe what you notice about them.

_____

_____

• Write a program to draw picture 2, using only the commands **fd** and **rt 90**.

_____

_____

A quicker way would be to use recursion.

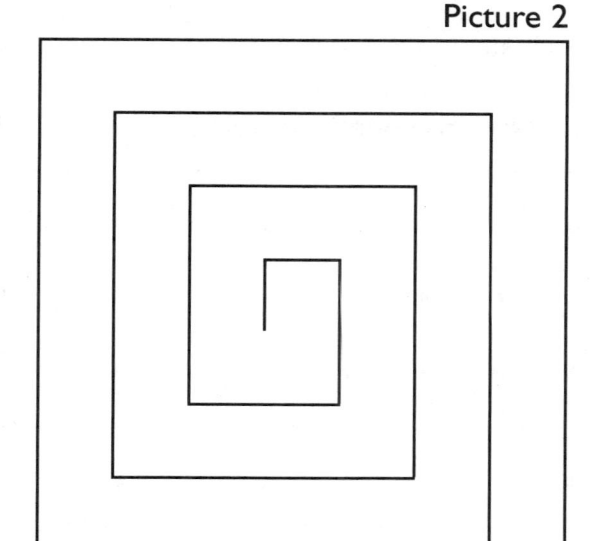

At the computer
✳ This time make a procedure called **spiral** in the edit box like this:

> **spiral 'length**
> **fd :length**
> **rt 90**
> **spiral :length+5**

What do you notice about the last line?

_____

_____

✳ Create the above procedure and run it by keying in **spiral 10** (press Esc to stop it!)

Why do you think the procedure keeps drawing?

_____

_____

✳ Make procedures that will draw different-shaped spirals.

ESSENTIALS FOR INFORMATION TECHNOLOGY:
Control through Logo

✹ Name _____

A superprocedure!

At your desk
✹ Write procedures for each letter of your first name (you may need to shorten it).

At the computer
✹ Now write a superprocedure that includes all of the below and call it **myname.**

✹ Test your superprocedure.

✹ ESSENTIALS FOR INFORMATION TECHNOLOGY:
Control through Logo

Superprocedures

✶ Make a superprocedure for a flower using the procedures for the following parts. The first one has been done for you.

	Procedure	
Leaf	repeat 80 [fd 1/2 rt 1] rt 100 repeat 80 [fd 1/2 rt 1]	
Leaves		
Stem		
Bud		
Flower		

Investigate different flower shapes by varying the number of repeats and the angle of rotation.

✶ ESSENTIALS FOR INFORMATION TECHNOLOGY:
Control through Logo

✳ Name _____

Snow crystal designs

If you could see a single snow crystal through a magnifying glass you would see that it has six spokes and is usually symmetrical. However, each crystal will have its own unique design.

✳ Create a superprocedure called snowflake and design your own snow crystal.

Before you go to the edit box you may like to experiment first. Make sub procedures to use in your main one.

Remember your crystal needs to be symmetrical and have six spokes.

✳ When you have tested your procedure, print out your design.

ESSENTIALS FOR INFORMATION TECHNOLOGY:
Control through Logo